Preparing for Baptism

Preparing for Baptism
using The Book of Alternative Services

Robert Ross

Anglican Book Centre
Toronto, Canada

1993
Anglican Book Centre
600 Jarvis Street
Toronto, Ontario
Canada M4Y 2J6

Typesetting by Jay Tee Graphics Ltd.

Canadian Cataloguing in Publication Data

Ross, Robert Adair, 1954–
   Preparing for Baptism

ISBN 0-921846-54-1

1. Baptism – Anglican Church of Canada.   2. Anglican
Church of Canada. Book of alternative services.
I. Title.

BX5616.R68 1993   264-03′00971   C92-095337-9

For my father

Table of Contents

Preface

In the last twenty-five years the Anglican Church of Canada has seen an amazing change in its baptismal discipline. In most places a "christening" is no longer a cosy little ceremony restricted to the candidate and his or her family and friends, but is rather a public liturgical act that occurs as part of Sunday morning worship (usually in the context of the Holy Eucharist). In addition, there has been much greater emphasis placed on adequate preparation of the candidate or, in the case of infant candidates, of the parents and sponsors.

In response to this change in baptismal practice, many parishes have established educational programs to help better prepare candidates and sponsors for the sacrament of Christian initiation, and to involve more members of the parish family in the ministry of catechesis. These often take the form of a *baptismal preparation team* made up of clergy and lay catechists who work and pray with the candidates (or parents of infant candidates) and share their understanding of Christian faith and practice. Some Anglican parishes, especially in urban areas, are even beginning to offer a complete program in catechesis for adult candidates (and parents of infants) based on adaptations of the Roman Catholic Rite of Christian Initiation of Adults.[1]

This book is intended to be one resource for such baptismal preparation programs. In parishes or communities where there are very few baptisms, it may be used by the pastor (or other catechist) as required reading for the candidate or parents and sponsors; or, in parishes where a baptismal preparation or catechumenate program has been established, it may be used for group study and reflection in conjunction with other resources (film strips, videos, Bible study, etc.). It is certainly not intended to be a text book with ready-made answers; nor is it intended

---

[1] See John Hill's excellent book, *Making Disciples: Serving those who are entering the Christian life*, 1991.

to replace the ongoing personal contact and sharing that should be a part both of baptismal preparation and post-baptismal ministry to neophyte Christians.

Since conversion to Christ is a never-ending process in which all members of the community, both new and old, are continually engaged, it would be a mistake to give potential Christians the impression that baptism is a reward for learning certain truths. Yet, in most cases, faith is nourished through understanding. And as we move away from the notion of baptism as "innoculation against original sin," it is more and more important to help people clearly understand the importance of that to which they are commiting themselves (or their child) in Christian initiation. While this book is not, by any means, a comprehensive treatise on Christian initiation, it can—and should—be used as one possible point of departure for engaging parishes and other communities in the essential and ongoing task of baptismal catechesis.

It is my hope that this brief commentary on the baptismal rite of *The Book of Alternative Services* will be of some help to those who have been called to receive new life in Christ— both those who are soon to be received into the community of faith, as well as those of us who must constantly renew and deepen our baptismal covenant in Christ.

Robert Ross
St Thomas's Church, Toronto
Pentecost, 1992

Introduction

To begin to understand the Church's changes in the baptismal liturgy over the past twenty years or so, we need to have some familiarity with the origins of Christian initiation practices.

Let us, therefore, begin this journey into the meaning of baptism with two fictional accounts of how a baptism might actually have been experienced in the distant past: first, in the Jewish roots of the Church's initiation practices; and, second, in the early centuries of the Church's life. Then, let us compare these ancient experiences with a typical "christening" in the not-too-distant past of the Anglican Church of Canada.

Jerusalem about the year 10 B. C. E.
Your name is Priscus. You are a middle-aged man and a Roman citizen. You have lived in Jerusalem for the past twenty years working as a minor civil servant in the taxation office. A naturally religious person, you have become increasingly unhappy with the religion of Rome, especially since a crisis in your personal life—the recent death of your wife. No one seems to take religion or philosophy very seriously—people seem to have become cynical and simply "go through the motions" of the state religion without much conviction. The same is true of the different schools of philosophy.

As a result of your interest in religious and philosophical ideas, you have had many informal discussions with learned teachers in Jerusalem over the years (sometimes when you were supposed to be discussing taxes!). Finally, you have decided that—despite all the risks involved—you wish to be received into the ancient faith of the Hebrews.

After attending the synagogue services for a time, you are brought before the religious authorities and thoroughly questioned as to why you would want to become a Jew. Having convinced them of your sincerity, you enter into a period of intense instruction—for a year or more—in the Law and the Jewish heritage.

When you are deemed ready, you are asked to renounce your former way of life and repent of your sins. You then undergo the very painful experience of circumcision. Finally, you are brought to baptism. Standing naked before a river you make an act of loyalty concerning the Law of Moses and are then completely immersed in the water.

Coming out of the water you are *signed* as God's sheep, slave, and soldier with the Taw (T), the last letter of the Hebrew alphabet, symbol of the name of God.

From that moment, you know that you have crossed the Red Sea and entered the promised land with your people, accepting everything that it means to be a Jew—the hopes, the persecutions, the joys. For you this is truly a new beginning and an incorporation into a new life of faith which is radically different from the past.

Rome around the year A.D. 215

Your name is Prisca. You are the widow of a minor civil servant. Through your daughter you have come to know something of an illegal Jewish sect known as the *Nazarenes* or *Christians*.

At first you worried about your daughter's involvement in this group (she was possibly risking her life associating with these people), but—as you come to see the incredible change in her sense of well-being—you yourself become interested, finally to the point of wanting to join *the Way*.

Through your daughter, who vouches for your honesty and acts as your *sponsor*, you meet with a *catechist* and begin a three-year process which involves exorcisms, reading the scriptures, and learning some of the traditions of Christianity.

As a *catechumen* or *hearer* you are permitted to attend the first part of weekly celebration of the Lord's resurrection—although, along with the other catechumens, you must leave before the liturgy of the eucharist begins, for only those who have been fully initiated can be present for the holy mysteries of Christ's Body and Blood.

Towards the end of the three-year period, you are admitted

as a candidate for baptism, and begin an intensive period of instruction and preparation, marked by various ritual actions (more exorcisms, the laying-on-of-hands).

Finally, you come to the time of your initiation.

You bathe on the Thursday and fast on the Friday and Saturday before the baptism. On Saturday you spend the whole night in vigil with your fellow candidates and the assembly, listening to readings and instruction. At cockcrow, you are led to a great tank of water, where the *presbyter* (*priest*) offers a prayer of thanksgiving over the baptismal water, comparing it to the waters of the Red Sea, the water of the grave, the Jordan river, the water of Mary's womb, the living water promised to the woman at the well in Samaria, the healing waters of Bethsaida, the water from the side of Christ.

You, and the other candidates, then renounce your former way of life; you reject "Satan, and all his servants, and all his works." The presbyter anoints you with oil (like a Roman athlete anointing his body before entering the arena) and says, "Let all evil spirit depart from you."

You are then led by a *deacon* (or *deaconess*) to a large tank and totally immersed three times in cold water, each time being asked by the presbyter to confess your faith in God the Father, God the Son, and God the Holy Spirit.

After the baptism, you are anointed with the oil of thanksgiving (*chrism*)—similar to the perfumed oil that you and other Romans use after taking a bath—and the presbyter declares that you now share in the royal priesthood of Jesus the Christ (the *anointed one*).

Then, clothed in a new garment, you are led back into the midst of the assembly and receive a second anointing and the laying-on-of-hands by the bishop, repeating and making public the anointing which the presbyter had given in the baptistry a few moments earlier.

The bishop signs you on the forehead, "branding" or "sealing" you as Christ's own for ever. You then join your new brothers and sisters in Christ in prayer, exchange the Peace with them, and share in the eucharist for the first time.

You do not understand the meaning of everything you have gone through (many of the actions will only be explained later), but you do know—beyond any shadow of a doubt—that you are now part of a living body of believers which is mystically united with the risen Lord. And you know that your life will never be the same again. For you, and for everyone with whom you are now united through this sacrament, life can only make sense in terms of the death and resurrection of Jesus the Christ. Through your baptism, you are a "new creation," and there is no turning back from the path on which you have now begun.

Toronto, A. D. 1965

Your name is Priscilla. You and your husband Bob are a happily married couple just beginning your life together.

Bob works as a minor civil servant at the government offices downtown, and you have just moved from your small apartment near his work, to a larger house in the northern suburbs. You are in the final months of your first pregnancy and are looking forward to starting a family.

Finally, the baby is born: a healthy, little boy. After you get home from the hospital, your mother-in-law asks if you have set a date for the "christening." You're not really sure about this since you are not really "churchy" (you attend at Christmas and sometimes at Easter), but since Bob's parents are very involved in the church you agree to let them arrange for the baby to be "done." Besides, you also want your child to be like other children and to be able to say that he has a "Christian" name! Bob suggests your sister be the *godmother* (even though she lives in Vancouver and won't be able to attend the service), and asks his brother and cousin to be *godfathers*.

The "christening" is arranged for the last Sunday of the month at 3 p.m. at Bob's parents' church downtown (the same church in which you were married). Bob suggests that the two families attend church at the 11 o'clock service of Morning Prayer that Sunday and then, after brunch, come back for the baptism— but you don't want to get a sitter for the baby, and putting him in the church nursery might soil the old and very fragile christening gown and cap that he will wear (a family heirloom).

Finally, the time comes for the service. The two families (minus the godmother) and a few close friends are present. The priest seems very kind (if a bit absent-minded) and gathers you all around the small wooden font in the baptistry at the side of the church. There is a silver bowl in the font with about a half-inch of water in it.

He hands everyone prayer books and then tells them which pages to turn to so that the responses can be made at the appropriate time (you rather wish you had read the service over before now— it's hard to know where you are supposed to answer, and you're not sure of the meaning of some of these questions).

The priest mumbles some prayers (in what sounds, to you, like "Old English"), reads a story about Jesus blessing little children, and then asks some questions about "the Devil" and the "sinful desires of the flesh" (you're not sure whether to join in with them or not, so you don't answer!)

After the Creed, some more promises by the godparents, and a prayer over the water, the priest says, "Name this child."

He repeats little Bob's name, along with the words of baptism, while splashing a few drops of water on the baby's head (and then immediately wiping the water off with a starched linen towel!).

He then makes a cross on the baby's head and says a prayer about him being "a soldier and servant." (Bob says after that he found this very moving, but you think it's a bit too militaristic!).

The priest then asks a whole series of questions, getting the godparents to promise to teach little Bob the Lord's Prayer, the Creed, and the Ten Commandments, and to make sure that he is eventually presented to the bishop for *confirmation*.

You notice that Bob's mother is looking very serious about everything that is happening, but the other relatives—especially the godparents—seem to have been caught a bit off-guard with the idea that "christening" implies some kind of responsibility or duty.

After the baptism, everyone says how good the baby was: he didn't cry once! Your mother can't get over how sweet it was when the minister kissed the baby after the baptism. Your mother-in-law seems strangely moved by the whole thing and is already talking about getting little Bob enrolled in something called Little Helpers.

You, however, are not sure what to make of this "christening." You couldn't really understand the prayers, and you're a bit disturbed at the notion of little Bob being "conceived in sin" (wasn't his birth the result of an act of love?). But you reassure yourself that, for the most part, none of this will really have much effect on little Bob. As long as he goes to Sunday school, your mother-in-law will be happy. Little Bob can make up his own mind about religion when he is twelve or thirteen—the time for confirmation and first communion. So, despite your misgivings about having to go through with something that you didn't entirely understand or even believe, you reassure yourself that you have done your religious duty as parent. There will be plenty of time for little Bob to make up his own mind about religion when he's older.

* * *

It would take even a very precise historian many pages to show how we have come from the Jewish baptism of Priscus, to the early Christian initiation of Prisca, up to the modern (and much diluted) "christening" of little Bob.

Some historians have suggested that the establishment of Christianity as the official religion of the Roman empire led to the assumption that everyone should be baptized as a matter of course; or, in later centuries, that an increased emphasis on the doctrine of *original sin* led to speculation about the fate of the unbaptized after death with a concomitant desire to baptize infants as soon as possible to save them from *limbo* (a cooler and more pleasant version of *hell*!). But, whatever the reasons, there is no doubt that, by the high Middle Ages, baptism had lost much of its original meaning.

The various revisions of the rite of baptism found in *The Book of Common Prayer* reflected the English reformers' attempt to restore the original meaning of baptism. Yet, despite their earnest desire to return to the practice of the primitive church, our sixteenth- and seventeenth-century Anglican forebears still accepted uncritically many of the assumptions of the medieval

Church and continued to see baptism as a kind of antidote to sin. This preoccupation set the stage in later centuries for theological arguments about the meaning of baptism, most of which centered on the philosophical problem of how splashing water on an infant can actually cause any kind of change.

Unfortunately, this kind of debate focused on only one aspect of the larger meaning and purpose of baptism, and still did not restore the much richer and more inclusive baptismal theology of the early Church. Moreover, the belief that the water of baptism was a kind of magical potion which guaranteed the salvation of souls was never really eradicated by the Reformation and, as we see in the story of Priscilla, it continues to linger on as part of the folklore of our own day and age.

The Book of Alternative Services deliberately attempts to recapture the richness of the earliest Christians' experience of baptism, and to translate that ancient experience of initiation into a rite that is meaningful to those who seek membership in Christ's Body in our own day. Of course, it is impossible for twentieth-century women and men to return to the earliest centuries of the Church's life and to experience Christian initiation in exactly the same way as our imaginary character Prisca. But the renewed rite of baptism is not—like an old movie or T. V. re-run—simply an exercise in nostalgia. Rather, it is an attempt to rediscover words and symbolic actions that express more fully the unchanging reality of what it means to be sacramentally initiated into the Christian life.

This kind of reform has, for Christians, always involved an attempt to return to our roots, that is to say, an attempt to rediscover the fundamentals of the faith and to translate those fundamentals into words and gestures that make sense to people in their own day and age.

For our imaginary friend Prisca, and for countless other actual Christians throughout the first centuries of Christianity, the experience of baptism was an unforgettable and life-giving beginning to a lifelong journey of faith in Jesus Christ. As you prepare for your baptism (or that of your child or godchild), it is hoped that the brief commentary in the chapters which follow will help you experience your initiation into the Body of Christ as an unforgettable and life-changing event. *Bon voyage!*

For Reflection

1. If you are a parent or sponsor of an infant or child candidate, spend some time thinking about your own baptism. What does it mean to you? Did it change you in any way? Give some thought to your reasons for seeking baptism on behalf of another person.
2. If you are an adult candidate, think about your own reasons for seeking baptism.
3. Re-read the three accounts in the previous chapter. What are some of the similarities between Jewish and Christian baptismal practices? What are some of the differences?
4. Using the three accounts of baptism (Jewish, early Christian, modern Christian) as material for reflection, try to articulate your own understanding of and feelings about the experience of baptism.
5. Is Christian baptism different from initiation into a group such as the Masonic Lodge or the Girl Guides? What are the differences?
6. Compare *The Book of Alternative Services* rite of baptism with that found in *The Book of Common Prayer*. What are the similarities? What are the differences? Which do you prefer? Why?

Chapter 1

Holy Baptism

Baptism is the sign of new life in Christ. Baptism unites Christ with his people. That union is both individual and corporate.

As we saw in the previous chapter, baptism has its roots in Holy Scripture and in the practices of the earliest (Jewish) followers of Jesus.

In the early Church, as we have also seen, baptism was (following the Jewish model) normally administered only to adults who would express repentance for their sins, as well as faith in the risen Lord, Jesus Christ.

Very soon, however, it became natural for whole households to convert, and the faith commitment of the adult converts was made "by extension" to infants and small children who were not able to answer for themselves.

Only later in the history of the Church did baptism come to be regarded primarily as "innoculation against original sin."

Sadly, this flawed understanding of baptism has lingered even into our own day (as we saw illustrated in the last chapter) with many parents still asking the church to "christen" their child because they are (consciously or unconsciously) afraid that, if the child should die, he or she will go to hell (or something like it).

The Book of Alternative Services rite, reflecting the most ancient practice of the Church, presupposes that a candidate for baptism is normally an adult seeking sacramental initiation into the Body of Christ, and that she or he intends—from that point onward—to live a life characterized by personal prayer, service to others, on-going repentance for sin, and regular participation in the eucharist.

Obviously, such a decision demands the maturity and intelligence required of any other major life-commitment. Yet, baptism is not simply like getting married or buying a house. As the *BAS* puts it, "to be a Christian is to be part of a new creation which rises from the dark waters of Christ's death into the dawn of his risen life. Christians are not just baptized individuals; they are a new humanity'' (p. 146).

It is because baptism joins us to something greater than ourselves that it may be extended to those who cannot (either because of age or for some other reason) make an adult profession of faith. Baptism is more than just an individual act; it is a sign of the new relationship between God and all human beings. A newly baptized baby is brought into that larger relationship, even though she or he cannot yet be aware of the fact. Again, as the *BAS* puts it, ''Becoming a Christian [has]... as much to do with learning to live a new lifestyle within the Christian community as it [does] with specific beliefs'' (p. 146).

Baptism is the beginning of a new way of life. And this is the principal reason why the celebration of baptism requires such careful preparation of all concerned—both for adult candidates, as well as for those (usually parents) who are seeking initiation into the Christian faith on behalf of an infant or child. Like marriage or ordination, baptism is just too important to enter into without adequate preparation as well as informed consent!

The church's renewed baptismal discipline does not always make people happy. Pastors are sometimes unfairly (and inaccurately!) accused of ''damning little children to hell'' by asking parents to examine their own relationship with Christ before commiting their child to such a relationship.

If, as a parent, you feel angry or confused by the church's renewed baptismal discipline, it is important to realize that God's love is offered to all people—not just to those who have been baptized. Baptism does not magically reserve for your child a place of worth in God's eyes—that place exists already. Rather, baptism will commit your child to an ongoing life of worship and service to others in the name of the risen Christ.

For Reflection

1. What is your understanding of a *sign*? How does baptism function as a sign of membership in the Church?

2. Look up some of the biblical images of baptism (Romans 6.3-5; Colossians 2.12; 1 Corinthians 6.11 and 12.13; John 3.5; Ephesians 5.14; Galatians 3.27-28; Titus 3.5; 1 Peter 3.20-21; 1 Corinthians 10.1-2). Do these images have any implications for your understanding of baptism?

3. What does it mean to be a member of *the Body of Christ*? Is *the Body of Christ* the same thing as *the Church*?

4. Do you believe that unbaptized people are "saved"? What do you think is meant by the word *salvation*? Should all people (not just babies) be baptized—even against their will? Are baptized people— even those who are evil or immoral—more acceptable to God than the unbaptized?

Concerning the Service

Any human activity—no matter how simple or complicated—needs some kind of plan. Whether one is cooking, or repairing an engine, or directing a play, some kind of overview of the ingredients, or the parts and tools, or the people involved is necessary.

This preamble to the rite itself, called Concerning the Service, is a kind of check-list for both the presiding minister and the candidates, and it provides a description of both the materials as well as the different "actors" and their functions in the "drama" of the service. What are these essential ingredients?

Concerning the Service immediately gives us the basic elements of baptism: words and water. These two things constitute the essential "outward signs" of the mysterious "inward grace" of baptism. The other *sacramental* elements—the signing with the cross, the oil of chrism, and the giving of the lighted candle—simply underscore the essential sacramental sign of water.[2]

Secondly, we are told that the ideal minister of the rite of baptism is the diocesan bishop. The reason for this is that—in the Anglican understanding of ordained ministry—a priest or other minister always acts "on behalf" of the bishop (who is the chief pastor of the diocese). The bishop, therefore, has a legitimate prerogative to preside at Christian initiation (and the eucharist) when he is visiting one of the many parishes which make up the diocesan family.

Thirdly, we are told that baptism has a unique and unrepeatable "character"—in other words, that something really happens when a person is baptized and that nothing can undo it. For this reason, baptism is a "once in a life-time" event which can never be repeated—a fact which makes it all the more important that adult candidates and sponsors of infant candidates enter the

---

[2] These actions will be fully explained in later chapters.

waters of baptism thoroughly prepared and with their eyes wide open![3]

Finally, Concerning the Service touches on the whole business of sponsors or—as they are often called—*godparents*.

The choice of a suitable sponsor is extremely important and needs to be carefully considered by every candidate for baptism, but it is especially important for the parent or parents of an infant candidate to reflect on the real meaning of sponsorship.

For instance, the custom of honouring a friend or relative by asking him or her to be a godparent—while full of good intentions—can have the effect of forcing an otherwise honest person to make promises that she or he really does not intend to keep.

For this reason, the preamble makes it clear that sponsors should be chosen not simply on the basis of sentimental or family reasons alone (although this might well be one factor). Rather, they should be chosen for the quality of their own faith and life.

Suitable sponsors need not be particularly ''pious''; nor do they always need to be Anglican. They should simply be practicing Christians who are willing to support the candidate as he or she begins the journey (and, in the case of infants, be willing to make the promises on his or her behalf). As the *BAS* rite puts it, ''Sponsors (traditionally called godparents) of infants present their candidates, make promises in their own names, and also take vows on behalf of their candidates'' (p. 150).

To ask a friend or family member who is not a practicing Christian to make solemn promises on behalf of your child would be unfair both to the godparent and the child!

Of course, in the case of infant candidates, it is most often the parent or parents who must take primary responsibility for the child's Christian nurture; they are the primary care-givers. But other adults can and should have a significant role in a child's religious development.

---

[3] Adult candidates who are not sure whether they have been baptized as infants, but suspect that they may have been, are ''conditionally'' baptized; that is, the presiding minister, at the point of immersion or pouring, says ''N., if you have not already been baptized, I baptized you, etc.''

When thinking about potential godparents for their child, parents might do well to consider friends or family members who seem likely to encourage the child's spiritual development through the example of their own faith and Christian practice. However, if no one seems to "fit the bill," they should not feel obligated to have sponsors. They should simply accept the fact that they will probably be the most important person in their child's religious development and, as such, will be the primary sponsors.[4]

A final word about sponsorship: in some parishes, especially those with many adult candidates, sponsors are often chosen from the congregation or parish family. Often such a parish sponsor studies and prays with the candidate during the period of preparation for baptism, and continues to support the candidate during his or her period of integration into the Christian life for a period of time following the rite of baptism itself. Such a *parish sponsorship program* may well be extended to the parents of infant candidates, who would often welcome tangible support and encouragement from a fellow traveller along the way of Christ.[5]

For Reflection

1. Why do you think the Church now asks that baptisms be performed during Sunday worship (especially in the context of the Holy Eucharist)?
2. What are your own feelings about being "received" (or having your child received) into a community?
3. What sort of qualities are you looking for in your (or your child's) sponsor?
4. Is it possible to be Christian without being baptized? Or, conversely, are there baptized people who are un-Christian? What does it really mean to be Christian?

---

[4] Some people have the mistaken notion that godparents must be chosen so that they can act as legal guardians if the parent or parents die before the child reaches adulthood. Legal guardianship is quite different from sponsorship for Christian initiation, and different criteria should be used to choose potential guardians for a child.

[5] See John Hill, *Making Disciples: Serving those who are entering the Christian Life*, esp. pp. 85-96, for a very helpful discussion of how to start a program for sponsors and catechumens.

Chapter 3

The Gathering of the Community

The purpose of this initial part of the rite is the same as at any celebration of the eucharist: to unite the assembled people as a community, and to prepare them to listen to God's word.

One of the complaints that many clergy still hear about the Church's renewed baptismal discipline is that it turns a "family affair" into a "public display." This criticism might make sense if the Church were nothing more than a collection of individuals connecting with God through direct, private lines. But the Church is, first and foremost, a community.

To be sure, each one of us is a unique and precious individual in the sight of God. But the Church does not consist simply of the sum total of every individual Christian. Baptism joins us, in a way that is ultimately beyond our understanding, to the Body of Christ—a community which unites all people of faith to one another and which extends through all of human history and even beyond the grave.

So it is primarily as members of a *community* of believers— and only secondarily as *individuals*—that we relate to God (which is not to say that God does not cherish our individuality, or that the Church should not value it).

For this reason, the Gathering of the Community is an essential part of the baptismal liturgy. Being (and becoming) a Christian can never be a private matter, and the Gathering of the Community reminds us of that fact.

For Reflection

1. Think of various gatherings of which you have been a part (dinners, reunions, surprise parties, thanksgiving, Christmas, sporting events,

concerts, etc.). What feelings have you experienced as you gathered with others for these events? Have you ever felt the same as you gathered with others for a church service?

2. "An isolated Christian is a paralyzed Christian." Do you agree with this statement? Is it possible to practice the Christian faith in isolation from other people?

3. Does the expression "private baptism" contradict itself?

Chapter 4

The Proclamation of the Word

This part of the rite is the same as at any celebration of the eucharist. Normally, the readings should be those which are proper to the day.

In examining the rite of baptism for the first time, adult candidates and parents of infant candidates might be tempted to take little notice of The Proclamation of the Word especially since baptisms normally occur on a Sunday, when the readings usually consist of the *propers* (that is, the particular portion of the Bible designated by the *lectionary* or *cycle of yearly readings*) for that day.

But even if the Sunday readings do not always refer specifically to baptism, The Proclamation of the Word is still an essential part of the baptismal service. Holy Scripture is our family story—the story of God's people, beginning in ancient times and culminating (for Christians) in the Good News (Gospel) of Jesus Christ, the Son of God.

As a candidate and sponsor begin to prepare for the celebration of baptism, there is probably no better activity than "breaking open" the words of scripture—that is, hearing the various stories in the Bible (especially in the Gospels) and attempting to mesh them with their own personal stories.

In doing this, we need not approach the biblical accounts simply as ancient "newsreels" from which we extract "facts"—in fact, such an approach would do violence to the intent of the evangelists and other writers of Holy Scripture.

Rather, we need to approach the Bible as a document written by people of faith and one which can only be fully appreciated through the eyes of faith. To open our own eyes to the truth and beauty of Holy Scripture is, therefore, an ongoing part of living the Christian life. And, in the same way, The Proclamation of the Word is an integral part of initiation into that life.

Sometimes, however, the proper readings for Sunday may seem really inappropriate for a baptism. Or, in parishes where "baptismal festivals" are held three or four times a year, special readings may be desired.

If this is the case, candidates (in consultation with the priest or other minister) may wish to choose from the list of readings that are especially appropriate for baptism (listed on page 165 of the *BAS*).

Whether or not these readings are used, a baptismal candidate or sponsor would do well to read through at least some of them, for they contain many rich images which relate closely to the symbols of Christian initiation. Some, or all, of these readings may also be used as the basis for discussion and reflection during the process of preparation for baptism [see *For Reflection* below].

For Reflection

1. Look up Ezekiel 36.24-28. List some of the images used in this passage. Do you think this passage has anything to say to how we might understand baptism? What are some of the "idols" that we worship in our day and age?
2. Look up Psalm 84, especially verse 5. Imagine that you are on a sun-scorched desert and there is a sudden cloudburst. What would you feel? Think of some of the "deserts" in your own life. Have they ever turned into "springs"?
3. Look up Romans 6.3-5. Try to connect what Paul is saying to your own life. What kind of "death" experiences have you had? What does it mean to "die to sin"?
4. Look up Mark 1.9-11. Is Jesus' baptism the same as Christian baptism? If Jesus was "sinless," why do you think he needs to be baptized? Mark understands Jesus' baptism as the beginning of his public ministry. Is the Church's understanding of baptism similar to or different from this?

Chapter 5

Presentation and Examination of the Candidates

Sponsors first present candidates who are old enough to answer for themselves. Parents and/or sponsors then present children who are unable to answer for themselves. The renunciations, in ancient threefold form, and an act of adherence to Jesus Christ as Lord and Saviour, then follow.

The baptismal liturgy begins, after the sermon or homily, with the candidates and their sponsors (and/or parents and godparents holding infant candidates) standing before the presiding minister.

Each candidate is presented by name to the presider, who then asks the candidate if he or she desires to be baptized.

This may seem an odd question —for, if the candidates did not wish to be baptized then why on earth would they be standing where they are? But it is essential that the candidates themselves be given the opportunity to express publicly their desire to enter the Christian Way.

In the case of the sponsors of infants or young children, the presiding minister asks the parents and sponsors:

Will you be responsible for seeing that the child you present is nurtured in the faith and life of the Christian community?

followed by another question:

Will you by your prayers and witness help this child to grow into the full stature of Christ?

Both questions are answered with the affirmation:

I will, with God's help.

This simple act of presentation is an extremely important moment and should not be omitted or down-played, for it is at this point that the candidate (whether adult or infant) stands at the threshold of a new way of life.

For an adult candidate, the significance of this moment may be felt much more if the presenter has, in fact, been a true sponsor—that is, a person who has had some part in bringing the candidate to this point in her or his life. Moreover, if the work of sponsorship (prayer, teaching by word and example, emotional support, etc.) has been done faithfully, then the words **I present N. to receive the sacrament of baptism** will truly be a high-point in the celebration of baptism, and not just a formality.

For a parent or sponsor of an infant or child candidate, the process of sponsorship will, of course, still be very much in its embryonic stages. And, for this reason, the presider will ask very specific questions about the parents' intentions to raise the child in the faith of Christ.

It is important to stress that, in asking parents to make promises on behalf of an infant, the Church is not merely asking them to do certain things—to promise to make a child attend Sunday school, for example, or to insist that she or he learn certain prayers or hymns or join the junior choir or servers guild (although all of these may well become aspects of a child's faith development).

The Church is really asking much more of the parents or sponsors of an infant candidate at this point in the liturgy: it is asking them to reexamine their own faith and ask themselves whether—in all honesty—their own commitment to the Christian journey is strong enough to enable them to carry another person until he or she can walk alone.

This is not meant to be some kind of inquisition or test. Faith in Jesus Christ does not mean having all the answers or even being "religious" in any conventional sense. It does not mean that Christians may never question the Church or have doubts about God—for doubt is always a part of deep faith. But it *does* mean making a commitment to the Christian Way: a commitment which can only be fulfilled in community worship and service along with other Christians.

The Examination of the Candidates concludes with a three-fold act of renunciation and a threefold act of adherence. The renunciations use, quite intentionally, the picturesque language of scripture, drawing on the biblical image of Satan as a reminder of the reality of evil in our world which is the result of rebellion against God.

In the ancient Church, this threefold renunciation of Satan was sometimes said by the candidate as she or he physically faced west as a sign of rejection of magic, superstition, evil, and all the works of darkness. Then, for the act of adherence, the candidate physically turned to the east—the direction from which it was believed the Lord would come at the end of time—to face the light of Christ.

These three renunciations, coupled with the three-part act of adherence, are beautifully summed up in the reaffirmation made by those who are already baptized but have come to renew their baptismal vows:

Do you reaffirm your renunciation of evil?;
Do you renew your commitment to Jesus Christ?;
Do you put your whole trust in his grace and love?

To this the candidate responds:

I do, and with God's grace I will follow him as my Saviour and Lord.

All of this gives us, in a kind of capsule form, the commitment which is asked of all baptized people.

Of course, if we really stopped to think about how difficult it is to live out this act of adherence to Christ, we might well never agree to such a radical commitment!

It can only be "with God's help," and with the support of other travellers journeying on the Way of Christ, that we can make such outrageous claims either for ourselves or for an infant.

For Reflection

1. Who is Satan? What do you think it means to "renounce Satan"?
2. What is sin? What are some of the "sinful desires" that draw human beings away from the love of God?
3. What does it mean for you to say that you will "turn to Jesus and accept him as your Saviour"?
4. How is it possible for an adult, on behalf of an infant, to "renounce Satan"?

Chapter 6

Prayers for the Candidates

Every liturgical celebration—whether it be the rite of baptism or the eucharist or some other sacrament—is essentially prayer, offered to God, through our Great High Priest, Jesus. Within this great prayer, however, there are also other specific forms of prayer and this point in the liturgy is one of those specific moments.

At this point in the baptismal liturgy, we pray especially for the candidates themselves. And it is in this kind of prayer—which is called *intercession*—where we present to God our hopes and desires for those who are about to be made members of the Body of Christ.

These intercessory prayers are in the form of a *litany* (which is from the Greek verb *to entreat*) made up of different *petitions* (or requests) which ask God to help the candidates to persevere in fulfilling the promises they have made (or which have been made on their behalf) and that—through the words and actions which will soon take place—they may be brought to the fullness of life in Christ.

Obviously, our petitions and intercessions are not simply attempts to tell God something new, or to convince God to carry out something that God would not otherwise do. Here, we are simply expressing our faith in the goodness of God and expressing our wish that our own desires and those of the candidates may conform to the gracious will of God.

True prayer does not consist of sending messages into "outer space"; rather, it is the act of trying to conform our human will to the gracious and generous will of God. In the Prayers for the Candidates, our request that God will bless and sustain those who are about to enter the waters of baptism expresses our faith in God's ability to do so. And, just as important, it indicates our firm intention to support the baptismal candidates in their new life in Christ in every possible way.

For Reflection

1. What is prayer? Is intercession (praying for others) the only (or most important) kind of prayer? Try to think of other kinds of prayer.
2. Take some time to reflect on the Lord's Prayer. Why do you think Jesus gave us this prayer as a model for all our prayers?
3. If God is all-knowing, then why do Christians bother to pray for other people and for themselves?
4. Why do you think most Christian prayers end with "through Jesus Christ our Lord"? What is significant about the word "through"? Is there any connection between prayer and baptism?

Chapter 7

The Thanksgiving over the Water

The Thanksgiving over the Water, similar in structure to the Great Thanksgiving prayer of the eucharist, recalls the waters of creation, the exodus, and the baptism of Jesus in the Jordan river. The prayer asks that those who are baptized may be buried and raised with Christ, cleansed of sin, and reborn by the Holy Spirit.

One of the most important things in our lives is water. Without water to drink, we would die; without water to irrigate plant life, there would be no food in the world; without water to wash ourselves, life would be miserable indeed! Water is not only a symbol of life; it is also one of the sources of life—an essential and most precious gift, and something we often simply take for granted.

But water can also be very dangerous. Anyone who has ever been in a ship at sea during gale-force winds knows how frightening and potentially deadly water can be. The same is true of anyone who has been pulled under water by a strong current or come close to drowning. Water is a source of life and of death. And the Thanksgiving over the Water is a kind of summing up of the power of this primal element in our lives.

In the Thanksgiving, the presiding minister prays that those being baptized will be cleansed and reborn—that they will share in the death and resurrection of Christ. This is not simply a pious wish; rather, it is an expression of the Church's faith that in baptism something really happens—that a human being is made a member of the Body of Christ.

Christians believe that the person of Jesus Christ has shown to humankind the fullness of God's love and mercy. But faith in Christ is not just the same as believing that there is a God, or even that Jesus is God's Son. Many people believe in some kind of transcendent or supernatural power. Christian faith, however, requires that we participate in the ongoing life of Jesus Christ as members of His Body (the Church).

This means for a Christian that everything in our lives—all the joys and sorrows that make up the fabric of human existence—must be seen, and can only be understood, as part of our participation in Jesus' saving death and ongoing life. The water of baptism is the outward sign of our share in Jesus' death and life—a sign of our death to the power of the old gods in our lives (selfishness, hatred, fear, and worship of power or worldly success) and our new and risen life in Christ—for in Christ, God has "come down" to share our human pain, even the ultimate pain of physical death.

The paradox of Christianity is that suffering and death cannot be separated from the new life that is promised to us in the resurrection. In fact, it is only by embracing our frail humanity, by abandoning our reliance on our own strength, and by accepting God's grace, that we can be reborn and refashioned into the kind of person God intends us to be.

The water of baptism beckons us to "drown" to sin—to face our dark side and acknowledge our poverty before God. For it is only by abandoning ourselves to God's mercy that we can be raised up from the dark waters of sin and death into the light and life of the resurrection.

For Reflection

1. Think of some of the different ways in which you use water in your everyday life. Try to imagine some of the life-giving as well as the life-threatening properties of water.
2. In your Bible, look up the first account of Creation (Genesis 1.1 and following), especially the part where the Spirit of God hovers over the waters. Do you see any parallel between this story and the Prayer of Thanksgiving in the baptismal service?
3. Again, in your Bible, look up the passage in Exodus where the children of Israel cross the Red Sea (Exodus 13.17-15, 21). How is baptism an exodus?
4. In baptism we are "born again" and "cleansed from sin." If this is true, why are Christians not perfect?

Chapter 8

The Baptismal Covenant

The congregation then joins with those who are to be baptized in the promises of the Baptismal Covenant. The Apostles' Creed, first composed for this purpose, symbolizes this covenant-faith.

In his book on the Apostles' Creed, Joseph Ratzinger quotes a story, attributed to the Danish philosopher Soren Kierkegaard.[6] According to the story, a travelling circus in Denmark had caught fire. The manager of the circus thereupon sent a clown, who was already dressed and made up for the performance, into a neighbouring village to fetch help, especially as there was a danger that the fire would spread across fields of dry stubble and engulf the village itself.

The clown hurried to the village and requested the inhabitants to come out as quickly as possible to the blazing circus to put out the fire. But the villagers took the clown's shouts simply as a good piece of advertising—something meant to attract as many people as possible to the performance. They applauded the clown and laughed till they cried. The clown tried in vain to get the people to take him seriously—to make it clear to them that this was no trick, but his pleas only increased the laughter. Everyone thought that he was playing his part splendidly—until finally the fire did engulf the village, and both village and circus were burned to the ground.

As Ratzinger points out, anyone who tries to speak today about Christian belief, especially as it is formulated in the historic creeds of the Church, must feel something like the poor clown in this story! Most people in our day and age are not very interested in creeds, other than those that we are given by economists, or scientists, or politicians. Our creeds nowadays tend to reflect our faith

---

6 Joseph Ratzinger, *Introduction to Christianity*, trans. J. R. Foster (New York: Seabury Press, 1969).

in free enterprise or medical science or western democracy, not in the reality of God in Christ. Like the people in the Danish village, the detractors of orthodox Christianity simply are unable to take the Church's claims seriously—they have heard it all before, and they know it has no bearing on anything that is really important in their lives. It's all just a comic routine.

If we are honest with ourselves, though, we must admit that the language of the Bible and the historic creeds is not a language that is easy for people in our day and age to understand; it needs to be interpreted or decoded if we are to get at the core experience of Christianity. Biblical scholars and theologians spend their whole lives struggling with the problem of how to translate scripture and doctrine into a language which is meaningful to modern people but which does not dilute the essence of Christian belief. But where does this leave the rest of us? How are we to understand the Apostles' Creed? Just what are we being asked to commit ourselves to in the Baptismal Covenant?

As we attempt to answer this question, the first—and perhaps most important—thing to remember is that baptism is not a kind of academic degree awarded to people who can somehow master the contents of the Christian faith. If that were the case, there wouldn't be many Christians in the world! Moreover, some (if not most) of the Church's greatest saints have been people of simple faith, many of whom could neither read nor write. So a high I. Q., or a degree in theology, is not a requirement for membership in the Church!

The word *covenant* itself may give us a clue to what is being asked of us when we commit ourselves to the Apostles' Creed, for it implies a *relationship* between God and humankind—a relationship which started with the creation of the world and which continues right up to the present time.

There is, of course, no possible way that we can somehow scientifically prove the existence of God or the meaning of his relationship to us; we can only experience it—just as the first Christians could not prove, but could only experience and attempt to describe, the resurrection of Jesus.

So when we commit ourselves to the faith of the Church in the Apostles' Creed, we are not simply accepting or rejecting this or that doctrine. First and foremost, we are commiting ourselves to a *relationship* with God through our membership in the Church—which is the community of all people who recognize and proclaim the fullness of God's love in the person of Jesus Christ.

The historic creeds were formulated at a time when the Church was struggling with the question Who is Jesus Christ? and when many different answers were competing for top place. The Apostles' Creed developed as a kind of shorthand summary of orthodox belief concerning Jesus—an attempt to state as briefly and clearly as possible the experience of the first witnesses of the resurrection.

This ongoing experience has continued to be expressed in different ways throughout the centuries since Jesus' death and resurrection, and the Apostles' Creed is only one way of trying to express our relationship with God through Christ (an earlier credal form was simply the expression "Jesus is Lord!"). However, because it expresses so succinctly the essential truth of Christianity, the Apostles' Creed continues to be a symbol of the totality of our relationship with God through Christ (which no words can ever completely describe).

The creed is not just a collection of doctrines—some of which we may or may not be able to "square" with our modern world-view. Rather, it is a symbol of the *totality* of the Christian faith. For this reason, the Church asks that those who seek baptism accept the Apostles' Creed as a sign of their membership in the community of people who, in every age, have experienced the reality of God in Jesus Christ.

* * *

The totality of the Christian faith, as distilled in the Creed, is expressed by the candidate's saying "yes" to the following questions:

Do you believe in God the Father?
Do you believe in Jesus Christ, the Son of God?
Do you believe in God the Holy Spirit?

In trying to understand what the Church is asking of us in these questions, we need to remind ourselves that we are not simply being asked to assent intellectually to three propositions (the way we might answer a skill-testing question in a contest!). Nor, as I said earlier, are we being quizzed on the total content of the Christian faith. What is being asked of us is really one question with three parts; and this question is not a test, but a kind of oath of allegiance to the reality of God.

This is not just a general kind of commitment to a vague notion of God as some kind of transcendent or supernatural power; rather, it reflects a very specific understanding of God as God has been experienced by Christians since the resurrection of Jesus.

Christians express their faith not only in God who is the Father, the Source, or Creator of the universe, but also in God the Son, who has saved humankind from the meaninglessness of evil and death; moreover, Christians believe in the God the Spirit —the invisible presence who continues to support and sustain us as we try to do God's will in the world.

The notion of God as Trinity would have been abhorrent to our Jewish forebears, who rightly stressed the unity and simplicity of God. But to the Jews who experienced firsthand the mysterious resurrection appearances of Jesus after his death—and who thereby became the first Christians—there gradually came the awareness that the fullness of God could be expressed only in this trinity in unity of Father (Creator), Son (Redeemer), and Spirit (Sanctifier). It is this faith—faith in a God whose unity is manifested in a trinity of persons—that the creed reflects, and which we, as baptized people, are called to reflect in our own lives.

Our faith in God the Father, God the Son, and God the Holy Spirit does not, of course, exist in a vacuum. Nor, as we saw earlier, does baptism simply establish a kind of "private line" between ourselves and God or give us some kind of special knowledge— far from it! The faith that we profess—and to which we are joined—in baptism is not a solitary or personal creed; rather, it is the faith of the whole people of God—a faith which encompasses people in every age and culture, and extends even beyond the grave (to what the Church calls the communion of saints).

Our profession of faith requires, therefore, that we "live out" our baptismal covenant in our everyday lives in the following ways:

— By continuing **in the apostles' teaching and fellowship, in the breaking of bread, and in the prayers**; that is, by following the authentic traditions given to us by the earliest Christians and by partaking regularly in the Holy Eucharist.

— By **resisting evil** and, when we are unable to resist, by **repenting**; that is, by expressing our sorrow to God and our neighbour when we have done something wrong, and trying to control our selfish and destructive impulses.

— By proclaiming **by word and example the good news of God in Christ**; that is, by drawing others to Christ by our own words and example, rather than trying to manipulate other people to be just like ourselves.

— By attempting to **seek and serve Christ in all persons**; that is to say, seeking to do good to everyone who crosses our path in life, not just those whom we like.

— Finally, by attempting to **strive for justice and peace among all people**, respecting **the dignity of every human being**; that is, by working to overcome our tendency to forget our common humanity, and ignoring (or despising) those who are different from us through race, gender or sexual orientation, culture, education, or socio-economic status.

These may sound like very lofty and perhaps unattainable ideals, and we may be tempted to become discouraged before we even begin the Christian Way—or to become disappointed or cynical as soon as we encounter a road-block or detour along the Way.

Certainly, in our faith journey, we will stumble and fall, encounter many dead-ends, and get lost on side roads. The promise of baptism does not guarantee an easy or painless life; however, it does assure us that, when we become lost and confused, Christ walks with us in our frustration and fear—leading us home to God.

For Reflection

1. Try to recall an important experience in your life. Write down as much as you can about that experience. Does what you have written completely "sum up" the experience? Could it be put in another way? Do the Bible and the Creeds say everything that can ever be said about the experience of being a Christian?
2. List some of your deepest-held beliefs. Can you prove that they are true? Have your beliefs changed over the years?
3. What is a metaphor? Do you think some, or all, of the language of the Apostles' Creed is metaphorical? If something is metaphorical, does that mean it is not real or true?
4. The word *spirit* means *breath*. How is God a *holy* spirit?
5. Read through the Covenant promises (which follow the Apostles' Creed) in the baptismal rite. Try to think of concrete ways in which you could live out these promises in your own life.

Chapter 9

The Baptism

In the celebration of baptism the symbolic aspects of water should be emphasized, not minimized. There should be water in quantity, enough for members of the congregation to see and hear when it is poured. An act of immersion would vividly express the Christian's participation in baptism, in the death, burial, and resurrection of Christ.

As we saw earlier, the Christian practice of baptism was borrowed from the Jewish custom of immersing converts to the faith in water (the word baptism actually means *dip* and in the early Church baptism almost always involved total immersion of the candidate).

In later centuries, as infant baptism became more and more common, the practice of *affusion* (pouring the water over the candidate) began to replace immersion—with the unfortunate effect of weakening the image of baptism as a "drowning" to the powers of evil in baptism, as well as a "rising up again" to new life in Christ.

In many Anglican churches—for architectural and pastoral reasons—total immersion of baptismal candidates may not be possible without a great deal of effort or imagination. But even if this may be true in many or most cases, the central importance of water as the symbol both of death and of new life should not be underemphasized.

For instance, rather than having just a small amount of water in the font before the service begins, the rubrics (or directions) of the rite of baptism suggest that water should be poured from a large pitcher or ewer into the font just before the Thanksgiving over the Water.

Candidates (or parents of infant candidates) have every right to insist that this essential action not be minimized or rushed through. Furthermore, it is quite appropriate to have lots of splashing of water. After all, this is not simply a quaint little ceremony—a "naming" or "dedication"; it is a sacramental sharing in the death and resurrection of Jesus Christ!

Water is the essential "outward sign" of baptism, but we should not ignore the words that are said at this point in the liturgy, for they are extremely important as well.

At this moment in the rite, the presider says:

I baptize you in the name of the Father, and of the Son, and of the Holy Spirit. Amen.

In some of the early Christian rites of initiation, these words (said as the minister immersed the candidate three times in the water) were accompanied by a threefold questioning and affirmation of faith:

"Do you believe in God the Father?";
"Do you believe in God the Son?";
"Do you believe in God the Holy Spirit?"

Only later did this simple affirmation of faith, which took place before each immersion, develop into the more detailed Apostles' Creed which, as we have seen, is now said by candidates and congregation before the actual baptism.

This may seem to be merely a rather obscure, historical curiosity and of no importance to this discussion. But, if we are to understand this moment in the baptismal celebration as more than simply hocus-pocus, then it essential to understand the strong connection between the Apostles' Creed (*"I believe"*) and the sacramental action of baptism (*"I baptize you"*).

This connection should help us to realize that the baptismal "washing" and the words that go with it—far from being a spell cast over an individual—are indivisible from the faith of the *whole* Church. So the central action of baptism is not—as many imagine—simply a kind of tonic, administered solely for the benefit of the candidate. Rather, it is an outward and visible sign of the new relationship which all human beings now share through Christ's victory over evil and death.

* * *

When the candidates have been baptized, the celebrant signs them with the sign of the cross.

After the baptism, the presiding minister makes the sign of the cross on the new Christian's forehead with the words **I sign you with the cross, and mark you as Christ's own for ever.**

This practice derives, as we saw earlier, from the Jewish custom of marking the newly baptized convert on the forehead with the Taw (T)—the last letter of the alphabet—signifying the name of God.

For a new Christian, the sign of the cross being traced on the forehead is a powerful reminder that he or she is "marked for life" in at least two ways:

First, it is a reminder that our relationship with God cannot be changed in any fundamental way; only wilfull disobedience on our part can separate us from God and, even then, God waits patiently for our return.

Secondly, it is a reminder that we as Christians must continually "bear the cross"; in other words, we must constantly die to our own selfish inclinations, in order to rise to a life that is directed to God and to our neighbour.

The sign of the cross is rather like "God's signature" on our forehead. It is a reminder also that, in the Christian scheme, there is no resurrection without death—both the little deaths of everyday life (the pains we must bear as a part of human existence) and the final death that each one of us must ultimately embrace.

* * *

The optional use of chrism at this point restores one of the most ancient baptismal practices. Chrism evokes a rich variety of biblical images: the anointing of kings (1 Samuel 16.13), the royal priesthood (1 Peter 2.9), the eschatological seal of the saints (Revelation 7). Its traditional association with the Holy Spirit interprets baptism as the new birth by water and the Spirit (John 3.5). In a similar manner it interprets the name Christ, *the anointed one, and relates the baptism of each Christian to the baptism of Christ.*

After the signing the celebrant then prays that those who have been made new in baptism may display the gifts of the Spirit in their lives.

As the *BAS* tells us, the term *Christ* means *anointed one*, and anointing the newly baptized person with the oil of chrism is—like the sign of the cross—another strong reminder to both neophyte Christian and the whole community of what has just happened in baptism. The use of chrism (from which the word *christen* derives) reinforces the fact that in baptism, through the operation of the Holy Spirit, Christians are "sealed" or "marked" as Christ's own for ever. And, while in no way adding to what has just happened at the font, the chrism is also a sign of our share in the royal priesthood of the Christ, the anointed one.

As members of his priesthood, all baptized people share both in Christ's offering of himself in perfect love to God the Father and in his ministry of reconciliation to the world. This is accomplished by following Jesus' example and offering (as the Thanksgiving after Communion in *The Book of Common Prayer* puts it) "ourselves, our souls and bodies, to be a reasonable, holy, and living sacrifice" to God; in other words, offering our whole life—as sinful and disfigured as it may be—to a kind and merciful God. And, just as important, our priestly ministry is exercised when we mirror Christ in our own lives—that is, when we are living sacraments or signs of God's love to the world.

The priesthood of the baptized is not one of worldly power or privilege; rather, it is one of self-effacing service to other people. The oil of chrism is, therefore, a tangible sign to both the newly baptized and the whole community of their share in this ministry, and their obligation to serve others in the name of Christ.

The concluding prayer, which immediately follows the signing with the cross and anointing with chrism, appropriately thanks God for bestowing upon the baptized the forgiveness of sin and raising them to the new life of grace; moreover, it asks that the Holy Spirit not only sustain the new Christians in their journey just begun, but also give them the gifts of the Spirit: joy, wonder, an inquiring and discerning heart, and the knowledge and love of God—all the good things which are available to those who have died to self and risen to the new life in Christ.

For Reflection

1. If baptism involves "death," then what is there to celebrate?
2. The sign of the cross is a sign of death by a particularly dreadful form of execution (crucifixion). Why is it also a sign of joy and hope?
3. What is the meaning of *priesthood*? How does baptism make every Christian a *priest*? Is the priesthood of all the baptized different from the ordained priesthood? If so, what are the differences?
4. Look closely at the prayer which is said over the newly baptized persons (*BAS*, p. 160). What is being asked? What are some of the ways in which the baptized (i.e., Christians) are "sustained" in their journey of faith?

Chapter 10

The Giving of the Light, the Welcoming, and the Peace

The newly baptized persons may be presented with a lighted candle as a sign of their new life in Jesus Christ, the light of the world.

Many parishes in the Anglican Church of Canada now fully observe the services of the *Paschal Triduum*: that is, the continuous liturgical celebration of the Lord's passion and resurrection from Maundy Thursday to Easter, including—on Easter eve—the Great Vigil, Christian initiation, and the first eucharist of Easter (see *BAS,* page 322).

Part of the Great Vigil of Easter is called the Service of Light—an adaptation of a very ancient liturgy which involves the lighting of the new fire (a symbol of rebirth) and the spreading of the flame to the large Easter candle and to smaller candles held by each member of the congregation.

The Service of Light culminates in the singing of the Easter Proclamation, which recalls God's mighty acts in history—especially his deliverance of the Hebrews from bondage in Egypt through the waters of the Red Sea—and his mightiest act of all: the resurrection of Jesus Christ:

This is our passover feast, when Christ, the true Lamb, is slain, whose blood consecrates the homes of all believers.

This is the night when first you saved our forebears: you freed the people of Israel from their slavery and led them dry-shod through the sea.

This is the night when Christians everywhere, washed clean of sin and freed from all defilement, are restored to grace and grow together in holiness.

This is the night when Jesus Christ broke the chains of death and rose triumphant from the grave. (*BAS,* page 324)

The Giving of the Light in the service of baptism is a kind of "mini" Service of Light recalling the Easter Vigil. (Of course, those lucky enough to be baptized at the Easter Vigil will experience the complete Service of Light as well as the Giving of the Light).

The small baptismal candle given to the candidate (or, in the case of an infant, the parent or sponsor) is lighted from the large Easter candle as a way of showing the intimate connection between Christian initiation and Easter; it is then passed to the candidate with the words:

Receive the light of Christ, to show that you have passed from darkness to light.

The Giving of Light reminds the new Christian (as well as the "veterans") that we have responsibilities as well as privileges as members of the risen Body of Christ; as the rite puts it:

Let your light so shine before others that they may see your good works and glorify your Father in heaven.

In baptism, Christians do not receive the light of Christ simply for our own personal salvation. Rather, we must show the light of Christ through the quality of own lives to a world which is often overcome by darkness.

It is significant that the rite speaks at this point about our "good works." The salvation given to us through Christ can, of course, never be earned by anything that we can do as human beings; it is a free gift from a loving and gracious God. Our new relationship with God through Christ demands, however, that we make a special effort to love and serve all people. Our responsibility as baptized persons is to seek and serve Christ in everyone, especially those whom our world tends to despise or ignore: the poor, the powerless, the homeless, the sick, people living with AIDS (the "lepers" of our own day); in other words, we are to follow Jesus' example, and act with compassion towards even the least of our brothers and sisters—not simply people we admire or of whom we approve.

We may not be able to bring ourselves to like everyone whom we encounter in our lives; but our baptismal covenant does demand that we try (with God's help) to respect the dignity of every human being and—as much as possible given our circumstances—to work for her or his well-being.

How we do this will be expressed in different ways, for we all have different opportunities for service in our lives. But for Christians there can be no escape from the world, no thought of a life lived in isolation from the problems of our fellow human beings.

As Jesus embraced the world—and in his vulnerability and openness to others was nailed to the cross—so we must embrace the difficulties and problems of our own "worlds," if we are to "shine before others" and, thereby, glorify God.

* * *

The congregation welcomes the new members of the community and urges them to confess the faith of Christ crucified, proclaim his resurrection, and share in his eternal priesthood.

The service then continues with the Peace.

Probably none of the changes in the liturgy has caused quite so much anxiety—nor so much misunderstanding—as the exchange of the Peace. Why—some people ask—is the exchange of the Peace considered such an important part of the renewed liturgy? Why can't we just *pray* in peace without having to touch anyone?

There are numerous references to the exchange of the Peace of Christ in the New Testament,[7] but the first clear evidence of such a liturgical exchange is found in early baptismal rituals at

---

7 See 1 Corinthians 16.20, 2 Cor. 13.12; Ephesians 6.23—24; Philippians 4.21; 1 Thessalonians 5.26; 2 Thess. 3.16; 1 Timothy 6.20; 2 Timothy 4.22; Titus 3.15; Philemon 25; Hebrews 13.24; 1 Peter 5.12; 3 John 15.

the point where the newly baptized were welcomed into the believing community. So the exchange of the Peace has its roots in a gesture of welcoming—a gesture which should be quite natural to human beings.

Yet, the meaning of the Peace cannot be limited simply to the notion of welcoming. Before the newly baptized person exchanges the Peace with his or her fellow Christians, the congregation says:

We receive you into the household of God.
Confess the faith of Christ crucified,
proclaim his resurrection,
and share with us in his eternal priesthood.

Just as the Peace is more than simply a friendly exchange, the welcome that we offer a new Christian is based on a reality which is deeper than mere human fellowship. The community of faith to which we welcome a newly baptized person does not define itself as a group of people who are necessarily friends, or who socialize together, or who even agree on every issue.

The Church—the "household of God"—is, indeed, a fellowship of human beings (and, in that sense, is a society of friends). However, the common bond between Christians is not based on what people today usually imagine as community—that is, a group of compatible or like-minded people. It is, rather, based on our common baptismal vocation which calls us to die continually to self and rise with our Lord to new life.

This is not to say, of course, that we should not try to be friends with our fellow Christians, or attempt to build strong communities in our parishes or elsewhere. But we need to remember that the foundation of Christian community is not necessarily found in shared activities or opinions; rather, it is found essentially in the new life that we have been given —and which we share—in Holy Baptism.

For Reflection

1. Look up Matthew 25.1-13. What do you think the wedding feast might symbolize? What is the "sin" of the foolish virgins? Can you see any connection between this story and the Giving of the Light in the baptismal service?
2. Consider the image of a *household*. Is a *household* the same as a *family*? Which word do you think better describes the Church?
3. Think about ways in which newcomers can be made to feel welcome in a community. How could the Church better involve both the newly baptized as well as long-time members?
4. Make an inventory of your gifts and talents. How are you using them for the good of yourself and others in the service of Christ?

Chapter 11

At Confirmation, Reception, or Reaffirmation

Confirmation, reception, and reaffirmation are various modes of response to baptism. Whether they involve making promises on one's own behalf, seeking membership within a particular branch of the Church, or reaffirming promises made long ago, each is directly related to the covenant made in baptism. The liturgy of baptism is consequently the primary context in which these renewals of the baptismal covenant take place.

Conversion to Christ is a life-long process. The sacrament of Holy Baptism makes us permanent members of the Body of Christ and, for that reason, it can never be repeated. But there may be moments in our faith journey when we will feel the need to reaffirm what has already happened to us in baptism. This is often particularly true for those of us who have been baptized as infants (at present, the majority of Anglican Christians), and who wish—at some point in our lives—to "own" our baptism. It is quite likely, as well, that a newly baptized adult may, at some point further on in the journey, wish to reaffirm his or her baptismal promises.

Whether this ritual action is understood as *confirmation* (in the various ways that Anglicans have used that word) or *reaffirmation*, the purpose of either action is fundamentally the same: to publicly recommit oneself to Christ and to ask for strength from the Holy Spirit to continue on the Way of Jesus.

While it is not possible here to discuss the history of what has come to be called "confirmation" in western Christianity, a few comments may be helpful in clarifying some possible misconceptions or concerns about the meaning of the renewal of baptismal promises.

First, it is important to remember that one is not baptized a

Christian in some general sense and then confirmed into the Anglican "faith."[8] There is, as one well-known hymn has put it, only "one Church, one Faith, one Lord"—despite our unfortunate denominational divisions.

In confirmation we do not "join the Church"—that has already happened in baptism, and nothing can ever add to or subtract from that fundamental reality.

But for Christians who have been baptized as infants, or who desire to reconnect with the community of faith after a significant absence, the Anglican church has long recognized the pastoral importance of providing an opportunity to publicly reaffirm the baptismal covenant. Moreover, the laying-on-of-hands, with prayer, is an ancient and powerful sign of the strengthening given by the Holy Spirit to help Christians live out their baptismal vocation.

For this purpose, the *BAS* rite provides three forms within a semi-continuous prayer: one for Confirmation, one for Reaffirmation, and one for baptized persons from other branches of the Church who desire to be received into the Anglican communion.

Such an action is, as we have already noted, *not* a repetition of baptism, but a strengthening of the good work already begun in baptism. As the prayer said by the bishop over the candidates for confirmation, reception, or reaffirmation so appropriately puts it,

Renew in these your servants the covenant made with them at their baptism. Send them forth in the power of that Spirit to perform the service you set before them.

The reaffirmation of our baptismal vows is, of course, accomplished every time we say the Apostles' Creed in church, every time we confess our sins to God, every time we receive Holy Communion, and in countless other less formal ways when we serve others in the name of Christ.

But the Church also offers us the opportunity to reaffirm

---

[9] There is really no such thing as the Anglican "faith." There is only the Christian faith, which the Anglican church has received and interpreted.

publicly our baptismal promise, at appropriate points in our faith journey. Such a public reaffirmation is not compulsory, and no Christian should ever feel coerced or manipulated into being confirmed. Like the other lesser sacraments (marriage, ordination, penance, and anointing of the sick), confirmation or re-affirmation is not an absolutely necessary prerequisite to living the Christian life fully. On the contrary, it is simply another possible means of grace—one of the many ways in which Christian women and men try to live out the meaning of what has happened to them in baptism.

For Reflection

1. What is your understanding of *confirmation*? If confirmation does not "complete" baptism, then what is the point of it?
2. Would it be appropriate for an adult to be confirmed immediately after his or her baptism? Why or why not?
3. Reread the prayer on page 160 of the *BAS*. If baptism consists of a "pouring out of the Holy Spirit," why would it be necessary to ask for God to do this again in confirmation?
4. How is *reception* different from *confirmation* and *reaffirmation*? Discuss your understanding of the meaning of these different terms.

Life in the Eucharist

The service continues with the preparation of gifts for the eucharist.

It is no accident that the compilers of *The Book of Alternative Services* put the rite for The Reconciliation of a Penitent immediately after Christian initiation.

Baptism may restore us to a new relationship with God through Christ, but it does not magically transform us into perfect, sinless people. It may put us on the "high road," but we must still make the journey—and that journey demands that we constantly deal with the weaknesses and limitations that lead us away from the path we are trying to follow.

As baptized people, we are not immune from this tendency to put ourselves in the place of God, to forget our need for God's love and mercy, and to start to see ourselves as completely autonomous and self-sufficient (as the popular song puts it: "I did it *my* way!").

One of the gifts that God has given us to live out our baptismal vocation—in spite of our sinful tendencies—is the sacramental life of the Church. And given our weakness as human beings, the new life that is offered in baptism can only be sustained by ongoing life in the eucharist. If we think otherwise, that is a sure sign that we are slipping back to the "I'll do it *my* way!" mentality—the mistaken notion that we can have a private religion which does not involve the community of believers.

But just as an infected finger or toe would affect the rest of our body, we, as individuals, affect and are affected by the Body of Christ. For this reason, corporate worship is not really an option for a Christian; it is an essential part of our spiritual health as members of the Body.

It is not possible here to get into the many different aspects of what it means to live the eucharistic life. Moreover, one could spend a lifetime trying to *understand* the eucharist—how it is that Christ is really present for us in the sacrament, what it means to be fed by his Body and Blood—and still not be able to *explain* what happens.[8]

While some understanding of sacramental theology can nourish our faith, it is important to remember that Jesus simply said *"Do* this for the remembrance of me" not *"understand* this." His promise is simply that he will be with us every time we break bread in his name. He did not ask us to spend our lives figuring out how this happens!

Adults sometimes worry about young children participating fully in the eucharist because they think children do not understand what they are doing. In fact, small children are often much more aware of the reality of Christ in the eucharist than those of us who are constantly preoccupied with how we can understand and, therefore, worthily partake of the eucharist. We are never really worthy of receiving the eucharist on our own; nor can we ever completely fathom this great gift. But, through our baptism into the death and resurrection of Christ, we are indeed *made* worthy.

To say that we are "made worthy" does not mean, as some think, that our fallen human nature is completely changed. We are still weak and sinful human beings who need the grace of God in our lives (whether we realize it or not). It is only because we now have a High Priest who intercedes to God on our behalf— one who has redeemed us and given us a vision of what our humanity can be—that we are made worthy to stand before the altar of God.

This gracious invitation to life in the eucharist is offered to all baptized people, not just to those of us who think we can understand the sacrament. We can no more understand the mystery of the eucharist in its fulness than we can understand why God would ever want to redeem us and make us worthy to stand before him. All we can do is accept this gift—with wonder, awe, and praise.

----

8 See John Baycroft, *The Eucharistic Way* (Toronto: Anglican Book Centre, 1981).

For Reflection

1. Why do you think the eucharist is so important for Christians?
2. Why is baptism necessary as "admission" to life in the eucharist?
3. Try to articulate your own understanding of what happens in the eucharist. Share your explanation with others, looking for similarities and differences. Does any one understanding of the eucharist exhaust its meaning?
4. "If we are not willing to allow infants and children to receive communion, then we should stop baptizing them." Do you agree or disagree with this statement? Why?

Other Christian Education Books from Anglican Book Centre

The Anglican Way by John Baycroft   0-919030-55-6
The Eucharistic Way by John Baycroft   0-919030-72-6
The Way of Prayer by John Baycroft   0-919030-79-3
This Is Our Faith: A Guide to Faith and Belief for Anglicans
    by Ian Stuchbery   0-921846-21-5
A Gift for the Journey: A Baptismal Preparation Kit by the
    Children's Unit of the Anglican Church of
    Canada   1-55126-044-1
*Exploring Faith and Life: A Confirmation Resource for
    Young People* by Barbara and Frederick Wolf
    Student Reader   0-919030-98-X
    Manual for Clergy and Leaders   0-919030-96-3
    Sponsor's Manual   0-919030-97-1
Life in the Eucharist: A Communion Program for Children
    by the Anglican Church of Canada
    Child/Parent Book   0-919891-46-2
    Leader's Guide   0-919891-55-1
The Gift of Life: Children's book for the Eucharist by the
    Anglican Church of Canada (for *Life in the Eucharist*
    program)   0-919891-62-4